A Ladybird Bible Book

Joseph

Text by Jenny Robertson
Illustrations by Alan Parry

Scripture Union/Ladybird

AF593664

Joseph had eleven brothers. Ten were older than he was and one was younger, but their father, Jacob, loved Joseph most of all. One day he gave him a beautiful long-sleeved tunic. The others were jealous and felt very angry with Joseph.

They were even angrier when Joseph told them about his dreams. 'We were all in the fields at harvest time, tying up sheaves. My sheaf stood up, and yours all came and bowed down to it,' he said.

'You're too big for your boots!' they snarled. 'You strut around in your fine new coat and think you can boss us about.'

'Well, my next dream's even better! The sun and moon and eleven stars all came and bowed down to me!'

Jacob overheard this and scolded his son, but the old man often wondered what the dreams meant.

Some time afterwards Joseph's ten older brothers took their father's flocks of sheep and goats to new pastures. Jacob sent Joseph along after them to take them food and to see how they were.

Joseph put on his fine new tunic and set off. His brothers saw him in the distance. 'Here's the dreamer! You can see him a mile off in that outfit. Now's our chance to kill him. We'll tell our father a wild animal ate up his dear little Joseph.'

'No, don't kill the boy,' said Reuben, the oldest brother. 'Just teach him a lesson. He certainly needs one! But don't hurt him.' So they agreed to rip off Joseph's coat and throw him into an empty well.

'Hello there, brothers! I've walked a long way with all this food for you!'

They crowded round Joseph, tugging at his new tunic.

'Hey, stop it! Leave me alone! Father sent...' Joseph began.

'Father's a long way away at home!' they sneered.

They tore off Joseph's tunic, beat him up and pushed him down the empty well.

Then they sat down and were just about to enjoy the food Joseph had brought, when they saw a line of camels coming slowly towards them.

'Traders on their way to Egypt!' they exclaimed. They hauled Joseph out of the well and, in spite of his protests, they sold him to the merchants for twenty silver coins. Joseph was tied up and led off to become a slave in Egypt.

The brothers killed a goat and dipped Joseph's torn tunic into its blood. They took it home and showed it to Jacob.

'Look, Father, we found Joseph's tunic,' they said.

'Joseph's tunic? Let me see. Oh, yes! It is his! It's my dear son's fine coat! A wild animal must have eaten him up!' the old man cried. No one could comfort him.

Meanwhile, far away in Egypt, Joseph was put up for sale in a slave market. The commander of the king's guard noticed how handsome and strong he was, and bought Joseph to be his slave.

At first everything went well for Joseph. His master, whose name was Potiphar, was so pleased with him that he put him in charge of all his affairs.

'Your God gives you success in all you do,' he said. 'With you in charge I don't have any worries at all!'

But before long things grew difficult for Joseph. His master's wife fell in love with him, but Joseph wouldn't take any notice.

Potiphar's wife was so furious she went to her husband and started telling lies about Joseph. 'Your slave attacked me!' she complained, and Potiphar believed her. He had Joseph arrested and thrown into prison.

It was a terrible time for Joseph. He had no friends to visit him, or to go to Potiphar to beg him to set him free. But God was still taking care of him. The chief jailer noticed him and was kind to him. Soon he had put Joseph in charge of the other prisoners.

Some time later Pharaoh, king of Egypt, was angry with two of his servants, his cupbearer and his chief baker. He had them put in the same prison as Joseph. The chief jailer made Joseph responsible for the new prisoners. One morning he noticed that they were looking worried, and they told him about the strange dreams they had had the night before.

‘I saw a vine with three blossoming branches,’ said the cupbearer. ‘Grapes grew on the vine and I squeezed their juice into Pharaoh’s wine cup.’

‘That’s a good dream! You’ll be set free in three days and get your old job back,’ answered Joseph.

‘Let’s hope my dream’s a good one, too!’ said the baker, cheering up. ‘I was carrying three trays of cakes on my head. All Pharaoh’s favourites were on top, but the birds flew down and ate them up.’

‘I’m sorry,’ said Joseph. ‘In three days you will be hanged and the birds will peck your bones.’

Three days later it was Pharaoh’s birthday. He set the cupbearer free and gave him his job back, but the baker was hanged.

Joseph thought that if Pharaoh knew what had really happened to him he would set him free. He had asked the cupbearer to tell the king about him but the man forgot. Two whole years went by and then Pharaoh himself had some strange dreams. He asked his wise men to explain them.

'I was standing on the banks of the Nile. Seven fine fat cows came out of the water and started to graze among the rushes. Seven more cows followed, but they were all skin and bones. The skinny cows ate up the fine fat ones.' The wise men muttered together, but no one could tell the meaning of the dream.

'This is my second dream,' said Pharaoh. 'Seven fat ears of corn grew on one stalk. Then seven thin shrivelled ears of wheat sprouted and swallowed the good grain.'

No one knew the meaning of the second dream, either. Then the cupbearer, standing at Pharaoh's side, remembered Joseph and told Pharaoh how he had explained *his* dream in prison.

'Send him here at once!' Pharaoh ordered, and so Joseph came and stood before the king.

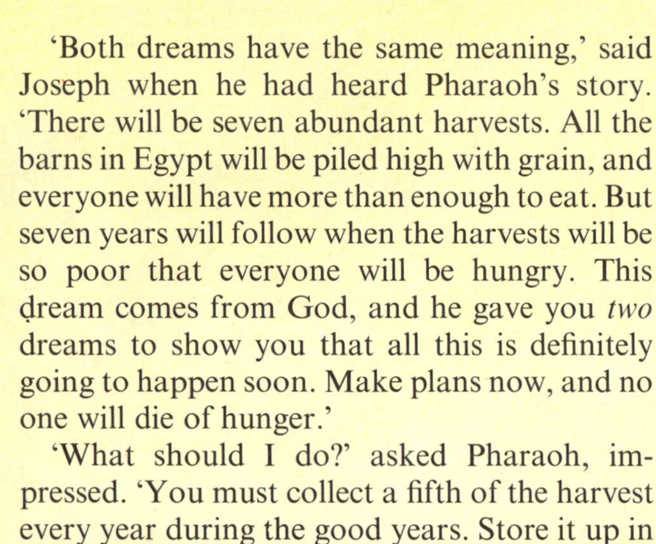

'Both dreams have the same meaning,' said Joseph when he had heard Pharaoh's story. 'There will be seven abundant harvests. All the barns in Egypt will be piled high with grain, and everyone will have more than enough to eat. But seven years will follow when the harvests will be so poor that everyone will be hungry. This dream comes from God, and he gave you *two* dreams to show you that all this is definitely going to happen soon. Make plans now, and no one will die of hunger.'

'What should I do?' asked Pharaoh, impressed. 'You must collect a fifth of the harvest every year during the good years. Store it up in barns and then, when the hungry times come, there will be food for everyone. Choose someone you can trust to organise it all for you,' advised Joseph.

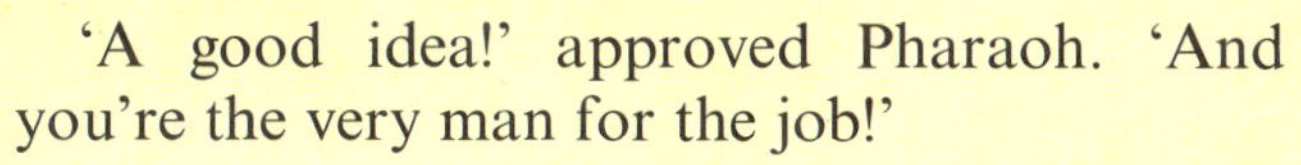

'A good idea!' approved Pharaoh. 'And you're the very man for the job!'

Pharaoh put his own ring on Joseph's finger and hung a gold chain round his neck.

'Now you're the most important man in Egypt, after me. Everyone will make way for you and do what you say.'

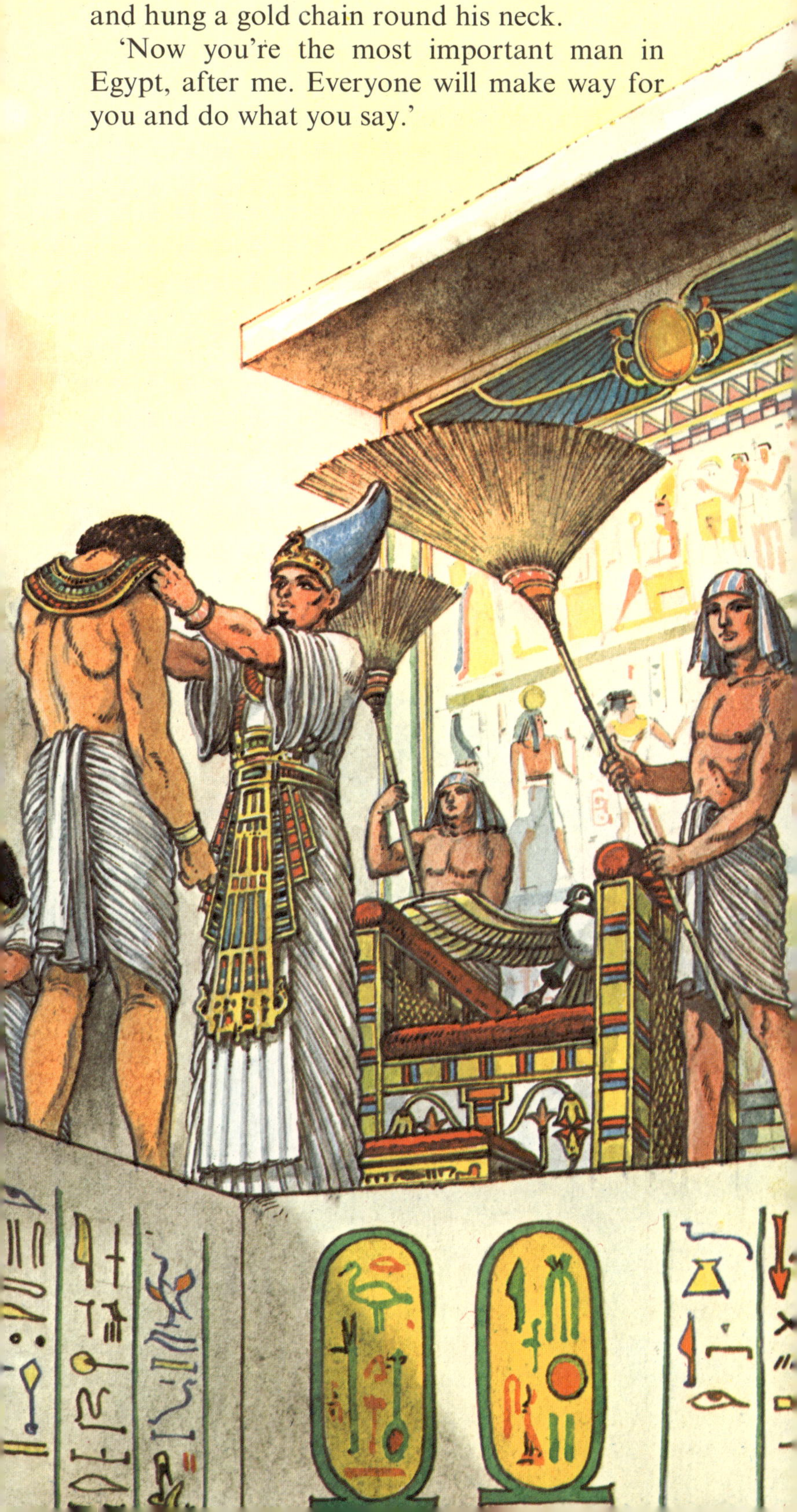

For seven years Joseph worked hard to build up enormous stores of corn. Then the first bad harvest came, and Joseph opened his stores for people to buy the grain so that they could make bread. The harvest was bad in other countries, too. Far away Joseph's brothers were running out of food.

'I have heard there is corn for sale in Egypt,' Jacob told his sons. He sent them off to see if they could buy any. Only the youngest, Benjamin, stayed at home. Jacob didn't want him to disappear as Joseph had done.

The brothers found the official in charge of the grain and bowed to the ground in front of him. They did not know it was Joseph, but he recognised them at once and remembered his dreams of long ago. He wondered whether his brothers had changed. Quickly he made a plan to test them.

'You're spies!' he challenged them. 'I'm not selling you any grain!'

'No, my lord. We are honest men, all brothers. Our youngest brother stayed at home with our old father, Jacob, who sent us to buy grain for our families.'

'Bring your brother here and I'll know whether you're speaking the truth or not!' Joseph ordered. He made Simeon stay behind as a hostage, but gave the others grain.

'We're being punished now for the dreadful thing we did to poor Joseph,' the brothers said. Joseph was very upset, but he pretended not to understand.

That night, when the brothers were on the way home, one of them opened his sack and found the money he had paid lying on top of the grain. To their dismay the others found that their money had been returned, too.

'That governor will say we're thieves as well as spies. He'll think we took his grain without paying for it. Whatever will happen when we go back?' they wondered.

When Jacob heard all this he was more determined than ever to keep Benjamin safely at home, but the famine was so bad they soon had to plan another journey to Egypt for corn.

'You must let Benjamin come with us this time, Father. That man will never give us any corn if we don't bring him along,' they argued, and Jacob finally gave way.

'Take the man presents: honey, nuts and spices; the best we've got. And give him back his money. It may have been a mistake,' Jacob advised.

So the brothers set off again with Benjamin.

When Joseph saw them coming he told his servants to invite them into his house for a meal. The brothers tried to return the money to Joseph's steward.

'Keep it,' he said. 'I was paid in full for all the corn you bought.'

He gave orders for Simeon to be brought out to them. Together again, but completely bewildered, the brothers waited for Joseph to arrive. When he came in they bowed down before him and gave him their presents.

'Is your father well?' asked Joseph. 'Is this the brother you told me about?'

Again he had to hide his feelings. He gave them a splendid meal and offered Benjamin five times as much food as everyone else.

Then, loaded with grain the brothers set off for home. Surely nothing could go wrong now! But Joseph's steward came chasing after them.

'Stop, thief! Stop! One of you has stolen my master's silver cup!' He searched through their things – and found the cup in Benjamin's sack. Miserably they all went back with him to the governor's house.

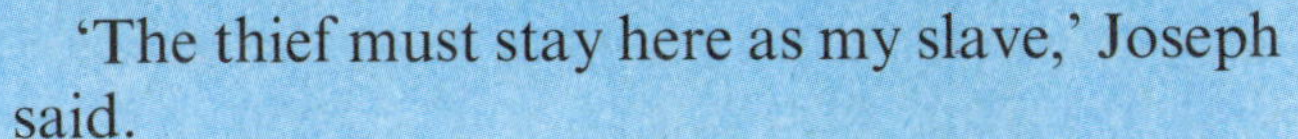

'The thief must stay here as my slave,' Joseph said.

'My father will die of a broken heart if Benjamin doesn't come home,' said Judah, one of the eleven brothers. 'Make me your slave instead, sir,' he begged.

Then Joseph saw that his brothers were no longer as cruel and jealous as they had been. He sent his servants away.

'Brothers, I am Joseph,' he told them, but they were too amazed and frightened to answer him.

'Don't be afraid,' he said. 'God turned the wrong you did to good. He has used me to save the lives of many people. Go and bring my father here to Egypt, so that I can look after him.'

When Pharaoh heard the news he offered new

homes in Egypt to Joseph's father and brothers. So old Jacob set out for his new land with his sons. Joseph rode out in his chariot to meet him. They flung their arms round each other and wept for joy.

'I can die happily, for I have seen you again,' the old man said.

'Don't talk about dying, Father!' exclaimed Joseph. 'Look, now all our family is together again. God has been good to us!'

He led the way to Pharaoh's court where he could provide all that his family needed.

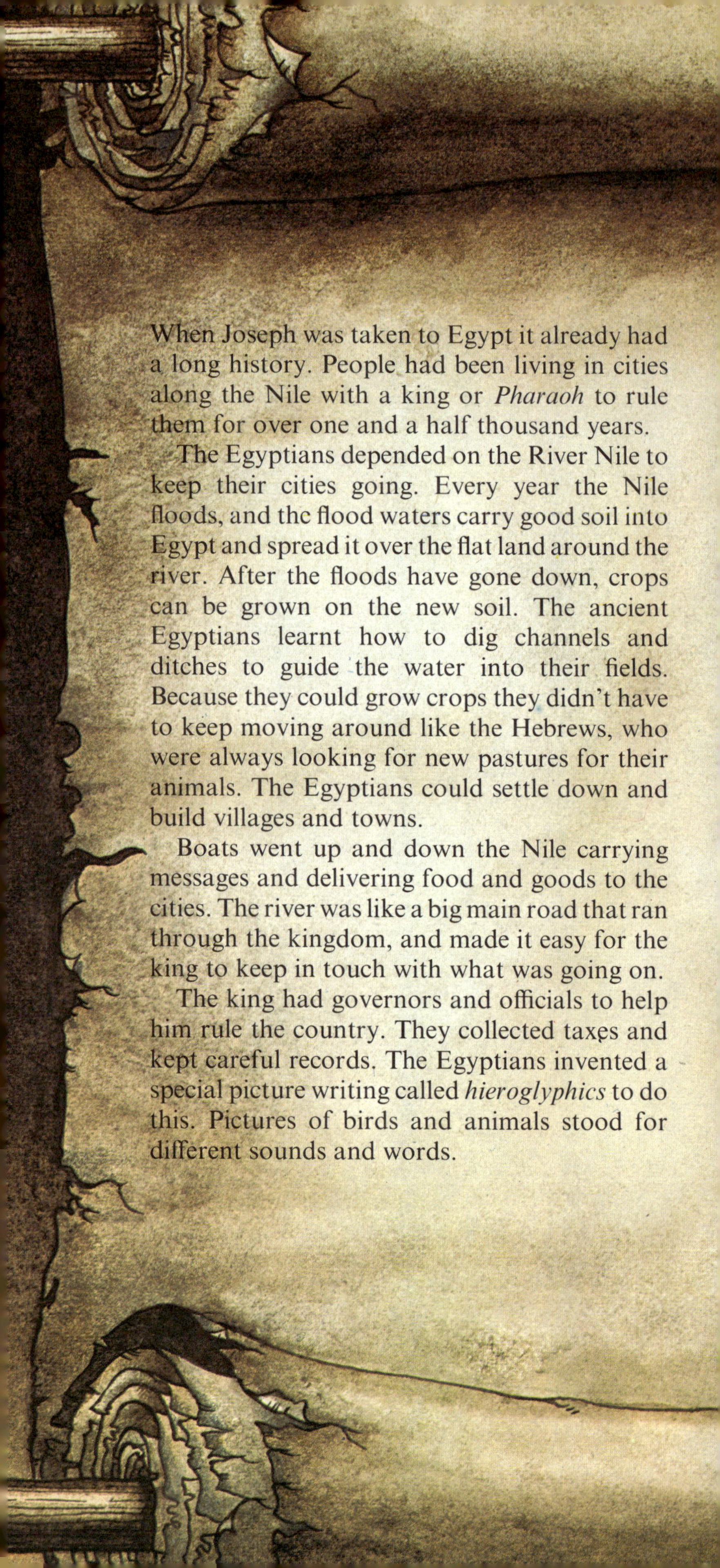

When Joseph was taken to Egypt it already had a long history. People had been living in cities along the Nile with a king or *Pharaoh* to rule them for over one and a half thousand years.

The Egyptians depended on the River Nile to keep their cities going. Every year the Nile floods, and the flood waters carry good soil into Egypt and spread it over the flat land around the river. After the floods have gone down, crops can be grown on the new soil. The ancient Egyptians learnt how to dig channels and ditches to guide the water into their fields. Because they could grow crops they didn't have to keep moving around like the Hebrews, who were always looking for new pastures for their animals. The Egyptians could settle down and build villages and towns.

Boats went up and down the Nile carrying messages and delivering food and goods to the cities. The river was like a big main road that ran through the kingdom, and made it easy for the king to keep in touch with what was going on.

The king had governors and officials to help him rule the country. They collected taxes and kept careful records. The Egyptians invented a special picture writing called *hieroglyphics* to do this. Pictures of birds and animals stood for different sounds and words.